A Voice in the Wilderness, volume 10

Winds of Change

Dalen Garris

DALEN GARRIS

This is a work of history. Historical individuals and places and events are mentioned.

Copyright © 2021 by Dalen Garris

Cover design by Renee Garris

Published by Revivalfire Ministries

ISBN 13: 972-1-7377944-4-8

All rights reserved.
No part of this book may be used or reproduced in any manner whatsoever, without written permission, except in the case of brief quotations embodied in critical articles and reviews, as provided by U.S. Copyright Law.

For information, address
dale@revivalfire.org

First paperback printing November 2021

Printed in the United States of America

"And he said unto me, Son of man, can these bones live? And I answered, O Lord GOD, thou knowest. Again he said unto me, Prophesy upon these bones, and say unto them, O ye dry bones, hear the word of the LORD."

Then said he unto me, Prophesy unto the wind, prophesy, son of man, and say to the wind, Thus saith the Lord GOD; Come from the four winds, O breath, and breathe upon these slain, that they may live."
(Ezekiel 37:3,4,9)

"And Elijah said unto Ahab, Get thee up, eat and drink; for there is a sound of abundance of rain."
(1Kings 18:41)

Table of Contents

1. Introduction — 1
2. A Thing Incredible — 3
3. New Generation — 6
4. Beauty from Ashes — 9
5. Where is their God? — 13
6. Keeping Her Candle Lit — 18
7. The Word of our Testimony — 22
8. Football and the Body — 27
9. What Happens When God Doesn't Answer? — 31
10. The Plague Has Begun — 35
11. Power in the Agony of His Blood — 39
12. Beauty — 45
13. A New Beginning — 47
14. Waiting in Zarepath — 50
15. Dragonflies in the Morning — 53
16. Thanksgiving — 56
17. A Torch in a Hospital — 60
18. Cognitive Dissonance — 63
19. Humility – the breakfast of champions. — 68
20. Christmas Gifts — 72
21. Inspiration to Keep Going — 76
22. One-Way Prayer — 79
23. Full of Surprises — 82

24.	Email from an African Evangelist	85
25.	Gideon	92
26.	Visitations and Ignorance	95

Introduction

There is a point in any revival when the direction of the Church changes and her focus shifts. This is the most critical point of the entire process because it determines whether or not the seeds of revival will take root or not. This is when the Church turns from being inwardly focused to being burdened with the desperate commission to win souls.

The Gospel is not about us; it is about others. When we finally realize that, we turn a corner toward the true focus of revival – the Great Commission. Our sails fill with the new winds of revival that blow us toward our destiny as we answer the call of the greatest cause of all time.

These winds of change never come easy for we are old winebottles set in our old ways. Repentance comes hard, but it has to be hard in order to be sincere. Obligatory altar calls will not do. Only broken hearts of desperate repentance will be enough to turn the ship around that corner.

Not everyone will answer the call. Only those who are willing to forsake everything. That is why true Holy Ghost revivals have been so rare throughout history. Few are willing to pay the price.

But there are those who do. It is those warriors who hear the trumpet, answer the call, and turn the Church into a new direction and a new destiny.

The winds of change are beginning to blow. You can feel the breeze across your cheeks. It carries the scent of Beulah land. We are heading in the right direction. We are almost home.

> *"Blow ye the trumpet in Zion, and sound an alarm in my holy mountain: let all the inhabitants of the land tremble: for the day of the LORD cometh, for it is nigh at hand; (Joel 2:1)*

A Thing Incredible

"Why should it be thought a thing incredible with you, that God should raise the dead?" (Acts 26:8)

Paul standing before King Agrippa is one of the strongest recorded witnesses there is. Here, in a temporary court set up for quick convenience for the king and queen is this young rabble-rouser whose fierce intensity and razor-sharp intelligence had once made him the up-and-coming star of the Sanhedrin. Now he stands defending his life in court as the mortal enemy of his once-proud sponsors. What changed? How did the pendulum swing from one extreme to the other to the extent that even his name was changed?

Paul met Jesus Christ of Nazareth, and they had not.

Faith is a funny thing. It can't be taught, forced, or manufactured. There is no secret place that you can find it hiding, just waiting for your discovery. It is not some whispered knowledge passed on through gnostic secret societies. All the elements for faith are right before all of us, easily obtainable if you reach for them. (Romans

1:20)

Faith is not believing <u>in</u> God or believing <u>about</u> God. It is <u>believing</u> God. Faith just is.

As Saul, the Pharisee zealot, he had all the necessary qualifications to be a great religious leader, but it was all built on a carnal faith. On the other hand, as Paul the evangelist for Christ, he was shattered to his knees by a great light that blinded him to the carnal and opened his eyes to the spiritual. He could finally see.

It seemed so simple to him now. King Agrippa, how is it that you do not believe? How is it that you cannot see this great thing that has come to pass but instead doubt the very things you believe are promised?

Because Agrippa is just like the rest of us. We believe what is convenient and set aside that which is not for some other time.

I believe that if we as Christians believed the Bible in every one of its aspects, its promises, and its judgments, how different things would be. Our days would be saturated in prayer and, instead of squeezing in 15 minutes somewhere, we would be clearing everything else in our day out of the way because we would finally realize how much power we had in prayer. The sick would expect to be healed because, instead of being too embarrassed to lay hands on someone, we would be searching for opportunities to heal the sick.

Our favorite pastime would now be reading God's Word, trading the disease of modern television for the anointing of the Word of God. Our hunger to read would increase as we begin to realize how much power, strength, and wisdom we continue to get as we read the Bible.

The specter of Hell would become real to us, and the desperate plight of humanity would drive us in a new passion and fury to rescue them before it was eternally too late.

In other words, as Paul admonished Agrippa, it would no longer seem incredible that God could raise the dead, but our faith would become real and we would become, not "almost persuaded", but changed.

New Generation

"According to their pasture, so were they filled; they were filled, and their heart was exalted; therefore have they forgotten me."
(Hosea 13:6)

Whatever happened to that Old Time Religion? The gospel I see preached in the churches today is not the same as the one that was preached fifty years ago. Something has changed, and there are fewer and fewer of us who recognize it.

I suppose that most of this new generation is glad that they are no longer part of what they may consider old, harsh, and strict. They lean away from what they consider legalistic, judgmental, and binding. The fear of the Lord, although acknowledged in precept, as it says in Isaiah 29: 13, has been upgraded, so to speak, to a message of Grace. Righteousness and holiness are now considered tenets of legalism and are spurned for a much gentler and kinder focus on a gospel of love.

Maybe God took some Anger Management classes in between the Old and New Testaments and has now changed the way He looks at things.

I have noticed some other changes also:

Sunday services are now more like a college lecture, complete with bulleted point presentations and prepared quotations. Gone are the impromptu messages that have no other source but a pure leading of the Holy Ghost. (Are we still allowed to say "Ghost?").

I have read of a famous preacher from those days who would stand silent behind the pulpit until the Holy Spirit fell down with the anointing. Try that nowadays and see how that goes over. Especially if that means services will delay you from getting to the steak house on time.

Those old-fashioned services were designed to change you so that you were not the same person you were when you walked in the door. Today, five minutes after you've crossed the threshold, you've forgotten what the message was about.

Back in those days, the whole church would gather together to pray down the Holy Ghost and would contend in prayer together until God moved. They didn't quit until they got an answer. Today, we're too polite to pray like that. I guess we don't want to disturb God if He's taking a nap.

I could go on, but you get the idea. If you're old like me, you remember. If you're part of this new generation of slicked-down seminary-educated preachers, you probably just think you know better than us crotchety old folks. Good luck with that.

Our society has changed. I don't know if our society changed our churches or if our churches changed our society, but they are most certainly linked together. If we want to return to a time of righteousness where God is once again sovereign in our country, we will have to change how we view the gospel and our walk with God.

And that starts with prayer.

> *"Thus saith the Lord, Stand ye in the ways, and see, and ask for the old paths, where is the good way, and walk therein, and ye shall find rest for your souls. But they said, We will not walk therein. Also I set watchmen over you, saying, Hearken to the sound of the trumpet. But they said, We will not hearken."*
> *(Jeremiah 6:16-17)*

Beauty from Ashes

It was 1969. The wind was blowing, the times were a-changing, and there was a psychedelic feel in the air. "Tune in, turn on, and drop out" was the cry, but underlying it all was an overwhelming desire to find Truth. We didn't know what Truth was, but we felt that we'd know it when we found it.

I found it in a little hippie church just off Sunset Strip.

I had not believed in God since I was a kid, but there was such passion in the eyes of the kid who invited me to come to hear "the Truth", that I just had to see for myself what had turned this longhaired hippie on to Jesus.

I knew something was different as soon as I stepped into the sanctuary. I could feel a presence in the air. All of a sudden, I knew. This was the real thing.

The Song Service was alive like nothing I'd ever seen, but it was the preaching that struck deep in my soul and made me realize that this was the Truth I had been looking for. I was at the crossroads of my life, and I went down to the altar and chose God.

We didn't have much. Basically, we had the

clothes on our backs, we slept on the church floor at night, ate potato soup or whatever donation they could scrape up, and didn't have enough money to buy a Coke, but it was the greatest time of my life! The Spirit of the Lord was there during the day and electrified the services every night. That was good enough for us. We would just read our Bible, pray like crazy for revival, and then go out and witness our hearts out.

All we had to wear were old t-shirts and ragged jeans with patches covering the holes. I guess we looked pretty scruffy and ragged to traditional church members. They didn't like our long hair very much, either. Said it was unscriptural and that we weren't really of the Lord.

I guess God didn't agree with them because He kept sending souls our way to get saved. Every night the altar would pack out with dozens of souls. From priests to prostitutes, housewives to drug addicts, and even some movie stars, God would send a new crop of Truth seekers every night to get saved and filled with the Holy Ghost. Over the course of 10 years, close to 100,000 souls were saved.

Despite the churches that looked down on us, there were some old folks who absolutely loved us. They were the old-fashioned Pentecostals that had been birthed out of the Azusa Street Revival there in L.A. They would come by and fuss over us and feed us fried chicken. It must have looked funny to see these old women with their grey Pentecostal buns and old calico dresses hanging out with us hippies. But what they saw in us was a resurgence of the Holy Spirit like they had experienced 50 years prior. We weren't dirty hippies to them. We were God's army that He was raising up to bring the gospel to a world that had been given over to sin. They made us feel like we were special. And I guess we were.

I miss those days. I have been rich and poor and have been all over the world, but I still remember those raw times when we had nothing but faith, a tattered Bible, and a handful of ragged gospel tracts. The Spirit of God set us on fire and we spread that fire around the world.

We may have looked like dirty hippies to the world, but to God, we looked like heroes. He took us from ashes and made us beauty unto Him.

"To appoint unto them that mourn in Zion, to give unto them beauty for ashes, the oil of joy for mourning, the garment

of praise for the spirit of heaviness; that they might be called trees of righteousness, the planting of the Lord, that he might be glorified." (Isaiah 61:3)

Where is their God?

"And these signs shall follow them that believe; In my name shall they cast out devils; they shall speak with new tongues; They shall take up serpents; and if they drink any deadly thing, it shall not hurt them; they shall lay hands on the sick, and they shall recover." (Mark 16:17-18)

I was dealing with some mistakes that I had made, thankful for God's conviction that caused me to stop and consider my impetuousness and impatience. I just really want to do what is right and not fall prey to my lusts, pride, and selfish desires. Thank God that we have the Holy Spirit to keep us in line.

And then I thought about how that much of humanity probably feels the same – we want to do what is right and pleasing to God (or our idea of some higher power). Everybody thinks that his or her view of reality is correct, while everyone else is slightly out of step. Some a bit more than others.

So, what separates truth from fallacy? How do we determine which one of us is correct? Church of Christ members won't associate with the Baptists across the street, Pentecostals feel sorry for everybody because they aren't as enlightened as they are, the Methodists are clueless of whoever is around them, the Episcopalians are buried in their liturgies, and let's not even talk about the Mormons, Catholics, and Jehovah Witnesses. We call Muslim extremists radical, but to themselves, they are just on fire for their God and are trying to do the extreme righteous thing, even if it means breaking the commandments of God to do it. How crazy is that?

Where does it end? It doesn't, because we are determined to grip onto our designated belief system in the face of all others. Why? Because we believe that is the one way for us to get to Heaven.

So how do we figure out who's right? Surely everyone cannot be right, otherwise, there would be no wrong, and by extension, no truth, no reality, and no great underlying meaning for life. As Einstein once quipped, "God does not play dice with the Universe". There has to be something that shows us what the right way is.

There is. It is the power of God.

Paul wrote in Romans 1:16 that the gospel of Jesus Christ is the power of God unto salvation – not the theory, doctrine, theology, idea, or calculated reasoning, but the power.

Is there the evident, palpable presence of the power of God in your church? Can you feel it, or do you just hypothesize that it is there? I am so tired of hearing that Jesus must be in the midst of us, "because the Bible says that where two or three are gathered together in His name ..." Is that all you got? Pul-lease! I want to FEEL the presence of God, not make believe I feel it!

Whatever happened to the outpouring of the Holy Ghost on your services? Do you even know what that feels like, or do you just talk about it as something that you imagine? When you step inside the front door of your church, can you feel that electrified feeling of the power of God? Do you feel like you are stepping into a cloud of holiness, and the chilling fear of God comes over you because you feel like you are right in the presence of God?

No, I didn't think so. If there were, there'd be a whole lot more going on at your church. You wouldn't be able to keep the crowds out.

What about the miracles? Gideon's response to the angel in Judges 6, when he was being told that God has chosen him to deliver Israel, was that talk is cheap. If everything the angel was saying was so true, THEN WHERE ARE THE MIRACLES OUR FATHERS TOLD US ABOUT?

When is the last time you saw the blind receive their sight, the cripple walk, and the deaf to hear? Please don't hand me that weak response about how God is going to guide the surgeon's hands. C'mon, if God is so powerful that He can stop the sun, why can't He heal the sick anymore? I'm not talking about gradual healing – I'm talking about immediate, miraculous, in-your-face, supernatural power right now. What's the matter? Don't you believe in that anymore?

Something is missing, and it is the power of God. *"These signs shall follow them that believe."* You are supposed to have real, tangible Holy Ghost power, and when you don't, you are no better than anyone else out there. Actually, you're worse, because you've been given this gift to distinguish you from the rest of the world, but you have squandered the grace of God and let it slip through your fingers.

So how do we figure out who is right and who is wrong? Through the power of God. It is the one thing that we have that no one else does, and God gives it to us to show the world that He is God. (Isaiah 43:10) But it is not free; neither is it cheap. If you are not willing to crucify your flesh, break your spirit and dive into the Spirit of God, then you will come up empty-handed.

Talk is cheap. When the real power of God is working in your church, there is no question.

And when it is not, there is no answer.

"Let the priests, the ministers of the Lord, weep between the porch and the altar, and let them say, Spare thy people, O Lord, and give not thine heritage to reproach, that the heathen should rule over them: ***wherefore should they say among the people, Where is their God?"***

(Joel 2:17)

Keeping Her Candle Lit

"...her candle goeth not out by night." Proverbs 31:18

What separates a nominal Christian from an on-fire Christian?

There is a line that God draws to separate those who make it into Heaven, and those who don't. I have often wondered where that line is.

I don't believe for a moment that just because I repeated a prayer of Salvation once in my life, that I am forever saved and can go on about my life living the way I please. Jesus didn't give His life so I could have an excuse to sin.

Neither do I believe that just because I believe God exists, or because I attend a church somewhere that I will meet the criteria that God requires. Jesus told those who claimed to have eaten and drank in His presence that He never knew them, even those who had prophesied in His name.

Let me go one step further and say that even perfection in doctrine would not give me entrance into that place of Grace that gives life to the soul. The Pharisees were squeaky clean in doctrine <u>and</u> works, but from the sound of things, they wound up in Hell.

I fully understand the importance of sound doctrine, which, as the building blocks for our house of safety, must be laid straight and true for the walls to be strong. The Apostle Paul fought fiercely to defend the churches against all sorts of heretics, including those who maintained that a return to circumcision and the works of the Old Law were necessary for salvation – a doctrine that is still alive today. And yet, while utterly important in directing our walk in God, correct doctrine can only point the way in which to walk, and works can only embellish it.

Something more is needed.

When reading about the virtuous woman in Proverbs 31, who is the picture of the true Church, I was struck by the passage quoted above. Who burns their candle all night long? And why would you do that?

I dare say that most of us turn the lights off when we go to bed. But not the virtuous woman. She kept her light burning throughout the entire night.

As Christians, we rejoice in our salvation and celebrate our transformation from Death, but a truly converted Christian will not stop there. He must look back into the darkness and shine a light so others can see the lighthouse of safety and come out of the world of death.

The essence of Grace is manifested in us when it transforms us from a creature of this world to someone whose heart and soul are planted in the next, and the realities of darkness become most stark when seen from that place of light. The dark seems darker and the despair seems more desperate.

We all have our testimony that we uphold, and while many are satisfied with that, others are not. Truly transformed believers are not satisfied with attending bland church services, fellowshipping with other satisfied believers in ivory halls of contentment, and warming ourselves with the coals of indifference.

Something inside us cannot rest while others are dying. While others seek the calm serenity of their chapels and cathedrals, there are those of us who want to set up a rescue station one foot away from the very Gates of Hell. Light the candle and let it burn all night long.

The Gospel of Jesus Christ is not about us. It's about others. Charity is what makes the difference between those who are content and those who are on fire. Charity is more than "love" – it is love in action. Above all things, even Faith and Hope, Charity stands as the essence of the entire Gospel, the main theme of the Cross, the whole reason why Jesus died, and the central reason of why we were called. Without Charity, we are but tinkling bells and a sounding cymbal – plenty of noise and pretty music, but lacking substance.

Charity is what separates the sheep from the goats.

The Word of our Testimony

One of the main issues that I emphasize in my Revival Meetings is the absolute necessity of winning souls. Revival is not about feeling good or having Spirit-filled services – it is first, last, and always about winning the lost. That is the true purpose for revival. Turning the focus of the Church off ourselves and onto saving others is the central theme of the Cross ... and one of the hardest things to get Christians to realize in their apostate churches.

Winning souls is so vital that I will usually spend an entire service on this one issue alone. I start with the last thing that Jesus asked us to do before He left – go make disciples. It seems we have done everything <u>except</u> what He asked us to do.

The Church of Ephesus in Revelations 2:1 sounds like a great church ... until you get to the part about leaving their first love (that love for telling others) and their subsequent demise if they don't repent.

The True Vine in John 15 tells us that if we do not bear good fruit, we will be broken off and thrown into the fire. Jesus says the same thing several times. What is that fruit? Souls. In

Matthew 21, Jesus cursed the fig tree because when He came looking for fruit, all He found were leaves. God doesn't want your leaves! He wants fruit! Where are the souls at your Altar Calls? Do you even <u>have</u> Altar Calls? When's the last time souls got saved at your church? Where is your fruit?

Just as marriage is a picture of our relationship with the Lord, so a wife is a picture of the Church. A church that is not winning souls is, in effect, a barren woman. Throughout the Old Testament, it is a shame to be a barren woman. In Genesis 30:1, Rachael cries out to her husband, "Give me children lest I die!" So also should our barrenness drive us to desperation in crying out to God. But, as is so often the case, it is one thing to know you are barren; it is another thing to care enough to have Rachael's Cry.

There are several other passages I usually bring up, such as the parable of the Talents, the Great Banquet, the Great Commandment, and several passages in Proverbs that revolve around the absolute necessity for us to show mercy on the lost. If we want mercy, we have to show mercy. And according to James 2:13, judgment will be without mercy on those who have shown no mercy.

There are several other passages that I lean

on, but my favorite is the Good Samaritan in Luke 10:25-37. Leading up to this parable, a lawyer asked Jesus how to escape Hell, and the Parable of the Good Samaritan was Jesus' answer. Here we have a man backsliding into sin -- going from Jerusalem, Israel's highest city, to Jericho, Israel's lowest city. Wounded by the devil, he was dying in sin by the side of the road. Both the priest (clergy) and the Levite (church people) passed him by because they didn't want to pick him up and help because they would get dirty and bloody. The Good Samaritan, however, poured oil and wine (the Anointing and the Spirit) into his wounds – in other words, he brought him to Salvation right there – and brought him to the church.

Now, what was the original question? Was it how to have a great church? Or become a good Christian? No, it was how do I escape the pits of Hell. Consider which of these three are going to Heaven, and which are going to Hell? How else can you read this?

Does that mean your salvation is based on your having mercy on the lost? Jesus said many would call to Him, "Lord, Lord" in the Day of Judgment thinking they were going to Heaven. But did they pick up the cross and follow Jesus to Calvary and give their lives so that souls could be saved? Or did they just spend their lives having "church"? There are some real serious issues here about serving the Lord that cannot be ignored.

James 1:22 says, "But be ye doers of the word, and not hearers only, deceiving your own selves." You can't just sit on a pew, hear the message, and believe in Jesus. You have to get up and do something, or else you will deceive yourself into thinking that everything is okay when the reality is that you are heading to an ominous surprise at the Day of Judgment, just like the goats in Matthew 25.

Another strong passage occurred to me the other day in the middle of a message I was giving. The Book of Revelations tells us repeatedly that he that "overcometh" will go to Heaven. Not he that "tries"; he that overcomes. And how do we overcome? By the Blood of the Lamb and the word of our testimony. In other words, 1) by the grace and power of the Blood of Jesus that saved us, <u>AND</u> 2) our testimony to the world of that saving grace. To testify means you have to open your mouth and tell the world about Jesus.

Oh, I know many will say that they let their little light shine in a corner and it is their good life that is a testimony to others. Get serious.

You are supposed to set your light out so everyone can see it, not put it under a bushel basket called Church. Testify is an active verb, not a passive one. Look it up. It means to witness. In one way, shape, or form, you have to be a witness.

The Great Commission you have been given as a Christian is to do as Jesus did – give your life so souls can be saved. It is the definition of Charity, the very essence of the Cross, and the heartbeat of God. It is why Jesus died. And it is essential if you want to receive the grace of God so you can pass over the Mercy Seat on the Day of Judgment.

> *"If thou forbear to deliver them that are drawn unto death, and those that are ready to be slain; If thou sayest,*
> *Behold, we knew it not; doth not he that pondereth the heart consider it? and he that keepeth thy soul, doth not he know it? and shall not he render to every man according to his works?"*
> *(Proverbs 24:11-12)*

Football and the Body

Some time ago, a retired pastor emailed me how he wished he could be serving the Lord like me out in the harvest field reaping all the souls. He felt useless, spent, and too sick and old to do anything anymore. The Lord gave me a rather terse answer to tell him that I was nothing more than a marionette on a string that was operated by the prayer warriors who were holding me up in prayer. It was the Prayer Warriors who won the battles. All I did was show up.

It strikes me how much it is like the game of American Football. No matter how good the Quarterback is, he can't win the game alone. While the Quarterback may control the play, his job is to pass that ball to others for the touchdown. It is the team that wins the Game.

In the middle of the front line is the Center. This is the Apostle that anchors the whole line, whose hands are first on the ball to hike it to the Quarterback. The whole team is centered around this guy who is usually the biggest and baddest player on the team. He starts the whole process going. How he starts the play is critical. If he does not hike the ball correctly, the whole play is over with a loss of yardage.

To the left and right of the Apostle is the front

line. These guys are always huge, muscle-bound monsters who dig their spikes into the ground, and are ready to do battle. You do NOT want to meet these guys in a dark alley. They will not give in, they will not back up, but will defend that line with every ounce of massive strength they possess. Rarely, if ever, do they get the Most Valuable Player award, and little credit is given to the battles they fight in secret, but without them, there will be no victory. These are the Prayer Warriors who stand in deep travailing prayer to hold back the enemy from charging in. No victory is ever won which has not first been fought and won in the prayer room by valiant warriors such as these.

Emmitt Smith, one of the greatest running backs of the game, after receiving one of the highest awards one season, spent hundreds of thousands of dollars to give an expensive gift to each member of the front line. His statement showed the character that made him great. Without those men on the line who blocked the way before him, he said, he would have never gained a yard, never mind win such a prestigious award.

Surrounding the Quarterback are the running backs – the Halfbacks and the Fullbacks. Their job is to do whatever needs to be done, offensively and defensively. If their job is to carry the ball, they will take it and charge straight into the line of battle. If the enemy gets past the Prayer Warriors on the front line they will form a defensive ring around the Quarterback to give him time to pass the ball, and they will guard him with their lives. These are the teachers, the deacons and elders, and the workers who labor behind the line of Scrimmage to make sure everything in the Church works.

And then there are the Wide Receivers, the evangelists and missionaries, running around out in the field, trying to dodge the devils that are dogging their heels, all the while yelling, "Throw it to me! Throw it to me!" The Quarterback has to know exactly when and where to throw that ball. If he doesn't do it correctly, the pass will be dropped and there will be no gain. Worse, it could be intercepted by the enemy and ran back for a touchdown. But oh! When that ball is sent sailing over the line, watch those Receivers dive for it like an acrobat, snatch it out of the air, and run like a racehorse for the end zone.

As the game progresses and the Owner of the Team watches from His box high above the playing field, the Coach calls the plays from the sidelines, encouraging and reproving and setting up every play. It is He that inserts each player into his particular role. It is the team that wins the game, not the players, just as it is the whole Body of Christ that wins the victory in this great battle of Eternity.

I may be one cog or screw in a huge machine, but I will fit perfectly in that place that God designed me for. I may want to have a more prominent place, a different job, or an easier task, but the machine will not work unless the correct parts are fitted into the correct place. Lord, I want to be all that I can be, but I don't want to strive to be something I'm not.

In the end, it is God who gets all the glory.

What Happens When God Doesn't Answer?

"Who shall separate us from the love of Christ? shall tribulation, or distress, or persecution, or famine, or nakedness, or peril, or sword? As it is written, For thy sake we are killed all the day long; we are accounted as sheep for the slaughter.
Nay, in all these things we are more than conquerors through him that loved us."
Romans 8:35, 36

Good question. What does happen when God doesn't answer? I'm not talking about causal prayer requests, but about those times when it seems like the whole world has collapsed around you and you are in such desperate need of a move of God that you are wrenching your soul out in prayer ... and nothing happens.

God doesn't answer every prayer -- that's pretty obvious – but isn't He supposed to pay attention when the stakes are so desperate that it becomes a matter of existence? And when He doesn't, is it because we don't have enough faith? Or are we not praying hard enough, or loud enough, or enough times, or with enough people? When God does not answer, why doesn't He?

The truth is that God sometimes sends you through trouble to test your mettle, try your resolve to stay the course, stretch and grow your character, and see if you will follow the Cross through the sufferings anyway. He sees things from a very different perspective than we do.

As we move into this modern age, we hear all these new "spiritual" movements that pull Christians like dumb sheep into new forms of faith and worship. These movements are not new but are as old as the Garden of Eden. It is the old story of telling people what they want to hear and tempting them with "special" wisdom, a new revelation, a secret knowledge that is designed to make you feel like you have entered into some higher level. You are lured by a Pied Piper into a path that is not the path of the lowly Nazarene.

It's an old lie that has been working ever since Satan sold it to Eve – "Hath God said? Thou shalt not surely die." That's what they believed at the foot of Mount Sinai when they worshipped golden calves that were more to their liking than that harsh, old Jehovah God.

And so it is today. These New Age Christians

don't have a reason why God didn't answer you. They are so enamored with supernatural signs and wonders and with the blessings and prosperity messages of "feel good" ministries that they have left off to fear God. These New Age Christians will tell you that you should just immerse yourself in the anointing and the Spirit will take you there. Their message is based on prosperity, not sacrifice. It's all about blessings, never about the sufferings of the Body of Christ. It's all about miracles and signs, never about repentance and holiness. It's all about the Crown, not the Cross.

There are two paths before us that lead to two very different destinations. There is the wide and broad path that seems so easy and good that it is a wonder that everyone doesn't avail themselves of all the blessings you can receive down that path. You're told that if you choose that path, you can escape the kind of sufferings and tribulations that you are going through now. But there is another path that calls to your sense of righteousness and holiness. It is difficult, rough, and narrow. It requires you to strip away all desire for pride and comfort and riches of this world and to place your treasure in Eternity. It is a path that leads to the suffering of the Cross.

Not many will choose it, but you have, and now you face difficulties that challenge you to the very quick of your soul and you have to choose if you will continue to believe God.

I don't know why God has not answered your prayers. There may be all kinds of reasons why you are experiencing the valley you are walking through right now. This much I do know, however, that you will not walk down any path that someone has not already gone down before you. There are some big footprints there in the sand in front of you, and one of them is the Lord's.

I also know that you will not walk through your valley alone. He will be there even when you cannot see or feel Him – He is there.

Every valley has two open ends – the one you walked into and the one you will walk out of. You will come out stronger than when you went in, refined in the fire to be "meet for the Master's use", and purified as fine gold (2nd Timothy 2:21).

He does hear you and holds your prayers like incense before Him. He knows. There is a reason for what you are going through. And He has chosen you for that reason.

The Plague Has Begun

> *"And Moses said unto Aaron, Take a censer, and put fire therein from off the altar, and put on incense, and go quickly unto the congregation, and make an atonement for them: for there is wrath gone out from the Lord; the plague is begun. And Aaron took as Moses commanded, and ran into the midst of the congregation; and, behold, the plague was begun among the people: and he put on incense, and made an atonement for the people." (Numbers 16:46-47)*

Korah, Dathan, and Abiram had risen up against Moses and had been judged. Korah was from the priesthood and the other two were from one of the other tribes – this was a rebellion that came out of both church and congregation. The judgment that had come upon them had been dramatic and sure -- there was no wondering who was right or wrong – and yet it had not satisfied the people. They wanted out from the strict religion of Jehovah, and Moses was the obvious target.

The very next day, the whole congregation rose up against Moses and Aaron and kindled the wrath of God. There would be no sweet-talking God out of this one. The pleas that Moses had used the last time were not going to work this time. God was mad.

There was only one hope. Send Aaron into the midst of them holding up the incense of prayer. It is the only thing that can stop the judgment of God once it has been determined. Prayer moves God.

Like so many others, I believe our nation has crossed a line, and I don't believe we are ever coming back. We are rolling toward judgment like a great stone wheel. The plague has begun.

The message we need today is a message of holiness and the fear of God, not a "feel good" message that skirts around judgment. It calls for brokenness, repentance, and a crucified walk in God, the Cross instead of the Crown, tears instead of blessings, and repentance instead of rejoicing. It calls for judgment in the earth.

Instead, I hear, "God hates the sin, but loves the sinner." Excuse me, but can you tell me where that is at, because I'm reading in Psalms 5 that He hates the workers of iniquity and despises them. He loved the whole world so much that He gave His Son, not that we would not perish, but that we <u>should</u> not. But He says in Proverbs 1 that if we refuse the fear of God and the way of righteousness, that He will laugh and mock at us when our destruction comes. I do understand that the Lord does not wish for any to perish, but for everyone to come to repentance, but there is also a limit to His mercy.

When we say that God loves the sinner, are we hinting at a more permissive Gospel than the old judgmental one that our forefathers believed in? Have we made our own golden calves as the Israelites did at the foot of Mount Sinai? Are we dumbing down the Gospel so that we can sound nice? Are we so worried about offending someone that we take no care about offending God when we change His Word and the very core meaning of righteousness?

The Word of God clearly says that God loves those who love Him, and that the love of God is determined by the keeping of His commandments. Over and over again, God tells us in His Word that love is the keeping of His commandments. He implores us in Jude to "keep yourselves in the love of God". How? By keeping His commandments.

God loved the whole world so much that He paid the ultimate price to give us the chance at salvation, paid for by the most precious substance in the Universe, His Son's blood. He had to sit and endure all those long hours as He watched His only begotten Son be tortured, beaten beyond recognition, and brutally nailed naked to a wooden cross ... for you. If you reject that after knowing the price that paid for your soul, is it any wonder that you stand in jeopardy of damnation and eternal fire? You can maintain that God still loves you if you'd like, but I would imagine it would be small consolation as you are plunging into the fires of Hell.

What are we afraid of? Why don't we call sin what it is? Why mollify judgment? Tell them the truth, for heaven's sake, and let them know they are headed to Hell. That is what real love is.

To smooth down the message with sweet-sounding slogans is not love, but is the very hate that you are so afraid of and keeps them from the repentance that would have saved them.

May we answer the call to stand boldly between the dead and the living, to proclaim the truth of God's righteousness.

> *"And he stood between the dead and the living; and the plague was stayed." Numbers 16:48*

Power in the Agony of His Blood

"Now unto him that is able to do exceeding abundantly above all that we ask or think, according to the power that worketh in us ..." (Eph. 3:20)

I went to pray over a friend of mine who was in serious condition in the hospital. We had prayed for him a couple of months ago when he was slipping over the edge into death, and the Lord answered mightily. I was on the phone with his wife as we were praying, and about 15 minutes into it, we both experienced the power of God come down in a finality that established the victory like slamming a standard into the middle of a battleground. It was done! God had answered!

Needless to say, the next morning, instead of dying as everyone expected, he immediately took a major turn toward life. Prayer had literally pulled him back from the dead.

I have seen just about every miracle healing I can think of from the blind, crippled, paralyzed, barren, broken bones, even one man who was virtually dead, but I still have no idea how it works. Or why. I have listened to all the theological experts explain how the whole process works, but I am still clueless. I can only step into the situation, lay hands and pray, and wait for God to do something miraculous.

And He does. Many times, an entire line of people who have come forward will get healed – every last one of them! But there are those times when you pray your guts out, and nothing happens. Burned into my memory is the picture of me in Africa holding a child that was brought to me with malaria. I prayed my guts out that morning, but, on the way to the hospital that afternoon, the baby died. You can't question these things; you just keep going and keep doing. God is in charge.

Despite all that I have seen, I am still intimidated and a little scared when I am asked to pray over someone. I don't know how it works, I don't always feel something when it does, and who am I anyway to drive my way into the Throne Room of God to demand this thing from God Almighty? This past weekend, however, the Lord was pressing me hard. Go and pray. Exercise the authority that I have placed upon you. Have the courage to believe Me and establish the promises that are planted in the Word of God.

Yikes! This has now taken a very different tack. This is no longer a mission of choice – this is a campaign of battle to establish the will of God. This is now a commission, not a request. The honor of God is on the table. He said it; we have done it; it is finished. Go!

And then the above scripture came to me. "Exceeding abundantly above all that we ask or think..." I get that part. God is sovereign. Everybody knows that. What has that got to do with prayer?

Ah, the "rest of the story", so to speak, is in the other part of the verse, *"according to the power that worketh in us ..."*

All of a sudden, this is not a work of chance or wishful thinking. It is not about tossing out some anemic prayer requests and hope that it works. And if it doesn't, oh well, it must not have been the will of God. No excuses, no backdoor exit, no nebulous theologies. NO MORE EXCUSES!

What did God say? Then have the courage to believe Him! As a friend once told me, "Act like you believe the Bible." That's it. It's as simple as that. Just step off the edge of the cliff and let God catch you.

The catch in this, however, is predicated on that one little turn of a phrase, "the power that worketh in us." This is not a free-for-all; there is a price to pay for the kind of power that God requires. This is not a matter of "works"; this is a matter of power. And we are required to do what it takes to get that power in God so that we can, in turn, exercise it so the world can see how great God is.

Wow. That stopped me cold. It's not just up to God – He's already there ready and waiting – it's up to us to go get that power in God so that this incredible power that is exceedingly beyond what we could ever imagine can work in us. That's how God works His miracles! Through us!

But we have to go get it.

I have said before that your place in God is determined by your depth of prayer. The oil for your lamps is gotten on your knees before God in deep, broken subjection. The deeper your prayer, the deeper you go into His bleeding side. That "secret place in God" that David speaks about in Psalm 91 can only be found in a place that is nailed to the Cross.

The troubles and pain in the valleys, the sufferings of the Cross, the crucified walks, the brokenness and surrender all lead to a place in God that cannot be found in the mountaintop experiences and pleasant times that we celebrate in church. This is the price we pay for that deeper walk in God. Pain and sorrow open wounds that take us into a depth in God that laughter never will. It also brings us into a walk of righteousness because the closer we get to God, the more we approach His holiness and are finally able to <u>understand</u> the fear of the Lord. Righteousness establishes the promises of God, and a crucified walk that takes us into the sufferings of the Body of Christ brings us to that place of righteousness, not because pain cleanses us, but because it opens depths in our soul that brings us closer to God.

Walking in this kind of depth establishes a confidence of faith and power in you that you never had before. It exposes your understanding to realize that time and space are not real. They are unrealities that tie us to this world. Only when you understand that time and space are not real will you ever be able to believe God for the impossible.

Walking in the power of God blasts demons, breaks chains, destroys obstacles, and heals the sick. God has given <u>you</u> power to heal the sick – He didn't ask you to ask <u>Him</u> to do it. He told <u>you</u> to do it. Now you understand; now you are empowered to exercise that which is "exceeding abundantly above all" because we have a power that works in us which has been forged in the fires off the altar of God – the same altar that accepted the sacrifice of Jesus Christ and that is covered with His blood.

That is where the power comes from – His blood on the altar of the suffering of the Cross.

But … you have to go get it.

Are you wondering about why things are so weak? Are you, like Gideon in Judges Chapter 6 wondering about where the miracles are? Why are our altar calls so empty? Why are services more like a college lecture than a supernatural experience with God? Where is the power?

It starts on your knees … and goes down from there. Power in God only comes from a depth of prayer that is washed in the agony of His blood.

Beauty

"And I took my staff, even Beauty, and cut it asunder that I might break my covenant which I had made with all the people."
(Zech. 11:10)

Of all things beautiful, nothing has any beauty other than what God has created in it. Flowers bloom in such incredibly gracious designs and gorgeous colors that it makes you wonder at the limitless imagination of the Creator. Sunrises and sunsets amaze us each and every time we see them, regardless of how many times we have viewed their display. How is it that our heart, mind, and soul can translate different wavelengths of light into such a feeling of grandeur?

And that's just the beauty you can see visually. What about the beauty of music? The mathematical symmetry of vibrations set against an orchestra can send your soul soaring. And what about the beauty of a loving touch, a physical tactile event that can translate into an emotion that exhilarates us. Or how about love itself, that emotion that has kept poets working for centuries trying to capture its essence with words.

Beauty is God-given, and as such can only be described in its own terms while it is expressed in so many ways. I imagine you might say that is it is the highest achievement of God's creation - that, and the ability He has given us to be able to perceive it.

As God's highest expression of love, Beauty took the form of a Savior who came to earth solely for us. There was nothing here that He came to enjoy or experience other than this one purpose – to save us from sin. Paul said in 1st Corinthians 13 that Charity does not seek her own, but bears all things and endures all things for others. Jesus was Charity incarnate, and He was broken for us.

When this grand scheme of things is over, we will look back on this life and finally realize how much God gave to call us unto Himself. His most wonderful creation, Beauty, was broken on the Cross so that we could have eternal redemption.

There is no greater love.

A New Beginning

> *"And being in Bethany in the house of Simon the leper, as he sat at meat, there came a woman having an alabaster box of ointment of spikenard very precious; and she broke the box, and poured it on his head..." (Mark 14:3)*
>
> *"Then took Mary a pound of ointment of spikenard, very costly, and anointed the feet of Jesus, and wiped his feet with her hair: and the house was filled with the odor of the ointment." (John 12:3)*

Simon the leper was probably the same Simon in Luke chapter seven who was also a Pharisee. Jesus must have healed his leprosy, otherwise, no one would have been allowed to enter his house – hence the party that he threw for Jesus and his disciples. How exciting to be washed clean of that awful disease and to be free again! No longer did he have to suffer the loneliness, pain, and suffering of being leprous. He had been cleansed from his sin.

Into the midst of this party comes a woman who is known throughout the community as a prostitute. She is probably the same woman that Jesus delivered from being stoned by these same Pharisees in John chapter 8. While the disciples surrounding Jesus probably had no idea of what was going on with this woman, the religious attending the party must have been aghast at her audacious entrance. Without so much as a nod to the host, she breaks an expensive alabaster box and anoints Jesus with a precious ointment. She then washes His feet with her tears and wipes them with the hairs of her head.

The alabaster box that she broke was her heart, and the costly spikenard she anointed Him with was her ointment of praise ... and the odor filled the room!

What a different response than Simon's! One in a celebratory dinner party hadn't even washed Jesus' feet; the other in broken-hearted humility of praise washed His feet with tears. There is a difference between thankfulness and praise.

Whenever there is a new beginning, there is an ending of something old. The depth of our reaction to that change sets the pace and intensity of our new beginning.

When we step into a new beginning with Jesus Christ, do we look back at the pit of sin that we were dragged out of with overwhelming thanksgiving and humble ourselves before our Savior in abject praise? Does the odor of your praise fill the room? Are you broken in humility before Him for what God has done for you? Or do we consider our salvation merely a change in religious status?

Simon was thankful, but Mary was transformed. Simon's new beginning lasted until dinner was over. Mary's will last into eternity.

> *"Verily I say unto you, Wheresoever this gospel shall be preached throughout the whole world, this also that she hath done shall be spoken of for a memorial of her." (Mark 14:9)*

Waiting in Zarepath

> *"And the word of the LORD came unto him, saying, Arise, get thee to Zarephath, which belongeth to Zidon, and dwell there: behold, I have commanded a widow woman there to sustain thee."* (1Kings 17:8-9)

I wonder what Elijah was going through during those three-and-a-half years of famine.

We don't know where he came from. He was a "Tishbite". Is that from the country of Tish? Where is that? Right next to Oz? Did he have a wife, a family, friends? Did he work at a regular job and all of a sudden was called to prophesy to King Ahab? Who was he, really?

All we know is that this old man who is a nobody coming from a place that nobody knows has the holy boldness to deliver an ultimatum to a very wicked king and command the powers of Heaven to stop the rain. Pretty impressive.

And then he runs away ...

This had to be a difficult time for him. He spends the next three and a half years in some foreign city with some widow woman and her son whom he hardly knows, scraping by with a residue of meal and oil that won't quit. Was there any word from God? Any sign of what was going to happen next? Did Elijah have any idea of what the plan was?

I don't think so. I don't think it mattered because this man walked in the depths of the fear of the Lord as evidenced by his pronouncement, "the Lord, before whom I stand". To know completely in the very core of your soul that God Almighty, the One Who created eternity, is standing right behind you constitutes a piercing of the veil of this reality that only comes from a very crucified walk in God, drenched in the chilling fear of God. That is where Elijah got his power from.

Three-and-a-half years waiting. Something has to be planted deep in your soul that tells you that God is not done with you yet. There may be no indication of what is coming, or even if anything is coming at all. You may feel like you are drifting on an endless sea with no sense of direction and wonder if He has forgotten you. He brought you to the dance, but has He left you on the dance floor all alone?

But there are those landmarks in your life that God warns us not to move. They are those experiences you have had with God that anchor the hope in our hearts that He is still there. He knows exactly where you are and what you are going through. When the proper time comes, He will move you into a position to fulfill that calling He planned for you so very long ago.

Did Elijah know? I don't think he had any idea he was about to bring about one of the great miracles in the Bible, but I believe he knew he was about to step into something. Did he realize the intensity of the coming battle to declare victory over the enemy and restore Israel back to God? I don't know, but if he was surprised, he sure didn't show it. He was too immersed in the power of God.

What do I do now?

You wait. He has given you a season to wait, to partake of the portion of the Word of God and prayer, the meal and the oil, and be ready for when He calls. He always does. He has not forgotten you, nor will He ever.

He is just getting you ready for the next victory.

Dragonflies in the Morning

I love mornings. I usually sit outside and pray on my porch at sunrise. As the rays of morning sunlight begin to peek over the trees, they cast a golden sheen across the lawn that glistens across the lingering evening's dew. As the morning sunlight starts pouring over the trees, it highlights the little gnats that are swarming around over the grass like a cloud of tiny pinpoints of light tumbling around in the beams of sunshine. There are thousands of them over the whole property, but they can only be seen where the sunlight hits them and lights them up like sparkles against the dark contrast of the trees that are still hanging on to their early morning shadows.

It doesn't take long before the dragonflies come. First one, then another, and soon the whole gang arrives for the feast - twisting, turning, and dive-bombing like tiny fighter planes in dogfights scooping up the little gnats, extinguishing the little sparkles one at a time.

This morning, however, the dragonflies had not shown up. There were gnats everywhere, but no dragonflies. I waited for the word to get out that the buffet was spread out and it was time to come and get it, but there was no response. So, I prayed.

I was having one of those quiet, intimate prayer hours with the Lord. We were so close that our hearts were touching each other. I love prayer hours like that. It is not a time for contending in battle or laboring in agonizing prayer, but it is a time of quiet fellowship with your Heavenly Father. He's right there, sitting next to you, listening to you pour out your heart in secret communion.

Since I was so close to Him at this moment, I thought I'd just ask for a little answer to prayer, "Lord, send the dragonflies." No big deal, just kinda for kicks, I thought it would be a neat thing to have Him answer such a small thing right while He was sitting there with me.

I waited. And waited some more. No dragonflies.

"Lord, You there?"

Still none. I went back to praying for a while, wondering if I did something stupid ... again.

After a while, lo and behold, what shows up but a single dragonfly. And then after 10 minutes, another one. By that time the morning mists were lifting and the day had begun. Soon they'd all be gone.

I wondered what the lesson was here. One

lesson I came away with was that, yes, God can and will answer even dumb requests like sending the dragonflies, but He doesn't always answer right away. Sometimes the answer has to come through a process before you are ready for the answer. And sometimes it is you that needs to go through that process. He will send it when it is time. We have to wait.

But the other lesson was that God is sovereign. He is not at our command to jump through hoops and roll over for us when we call. He is God and we are at His command, not the other way around. There are rock-solid promises in the Word of God, but every promise of God has conditions – nothing is free and rarely is cheap – but in the end, God is sovereign and will do as He pleases.

He did send two dragonflies, though. But he sent them in His own time, just to give me a lesson of faith and patience on a misty morning.

Thanksgiving

The book of Proverbs has an amazing ability to adjust to whatever message you need to hear on any given day. If you need encouragement, it will support you; if you need correction, it will reprove you; if you need wisdom, it will show you what you need to do to get it. You can read the same chapters over and over again, and they will speak differently to you each time, morphing into whatever you need at the moment.

Sometimes, it's as if the whole chapter has joined together in a conspiracy against you to drive home the day's message. Today was like that.

I was first pricked with, "a man of knowledge increaseth strength". Okay, I get it – I need to read more Bible. If I want to fight battles, win victories, or overcome struggles, I need to read more of the Word of God. When you forget your reading and prayer, you can forget your power in God.

Okay, so now I have been reproved – I have to read more. But that also tells me that something is coming up that I will need that strength for. Maybe a battle or maybe a mission;

either way, it's obvious that He is reminding me that there is something that I have to do and I cannot do it on my own.

Then a little more down the chapter, I came to, "if thou faint in the day of adversity, thy strength is small". I remember this one well. A few years ago, the Lord used this one to convict me about going to Africa on a particular trip. ("Okay, okay! I'm going!"). But that proverb was only setting me up for the next verse, and this one <u>really</u> got me.

> *"If thou forbear to deliver them that are drawn unto death, and those that are ready to be slain; if thou sayest, Behold, we knew it not; doth not he that pondereth the heart consider it? And he that keepeth thy soul, doth not he know it? And shall not he render to every man according to his works?" (Proverbs 24:11-12)*

Is that our default attitude when we are not being pushed or convicted? Do we maintain our status quo with, "I love everybody, and I sure hope they all figure it out and get to Heaven somehow"? We know multitudes are starving, not only for food and physical needs but, more importantly, for spiritual needs. Amos tells us in chapter 8 that God would send a famine for hearing the Word of God and men would travel everywhere seeking it but would not be able to find it. As chilling as that may sound, do we answer that challenge by questioning what we can do? Or perhaps, more like what we are <u>required</u> to do? Or worse, what the absolute minimum is that we can get away with?

Water seeks its own level. So do we. Left alone, we tend to slip into complacency when it concerns others outside our immediate circle. In other words, we become lukewarm.

And then the chapter conspired against me one more time to finalize it all at the end:

> *"I went by the field of the slothful, and by the vineyard of the man void of understanding; And, lo, it was all grown over with thorns, and nettles had covered the face thereof, and the stone wall thereof was broken down. Then I saw, and considered it well: I looked upon it, and received instruction. Yet a little sleep, a little slumber, a little folding of the hands to sleep:*

So shall thy poverty come as one that travels; and thy want as an armed man." (Proverbs 24: 30-34)

I get it. Life is a test. It is not about us and what we can get for ourselves by padding our own nest and keeping as much as we can, but rather, it is about seeing how much we can do for others with what God has allowed us to have. If we gave it all away, somehow I feel that our bucket would never be empty.

This Thanksgiving season, I want to stop for a moment and thank God, not just for what I have, but for the opportunity He has given us to give.

It's what God did for us.

"For he hath made him to be sin for us, who knew no sin; that we might be made the righteousness of God in him." (2nd Corinthians 5:21)

A Torch in a Hospital

I just came out of a minor surgery at Baylor Baptist Hospital in Dallas. Just a simple thing, but it required a few hours of recovery. I had a great time interacting with the nurses, cracking jokes, uplifting my wife who was sitting there with that look on her face that made me know that I must have looked like hell.

I can talk to anybody. Standing in line at the supermarket, sitting on a park bench, in the next row at the movies, almost anywhere people are easy to talk to. You just have to reach out and touch them. Even in a hospital.

When I had my heart attack 3 years ago, however, I was so in shock that I didn't consider all the other patients on my floor who also needed consideration. Even though the nurses were throwing fits every time I got out of bed, I could have taken some time to minister to the others who were there. We were all in a serious condition, but I had the Light of Life and I didn't share it with them. I came home pretty convicted for that.

Yesterday as I was getting prepped to leave, I shouted out, "Praise God Almighty, I am free at last!" The nurse hollered from across the room,

"I didn't know you were a preacher!"

I don't ever want to hear that again.

We overcome, the Bible says in Rev. 12:11, by the Blood of the Lamb and the word of our testimony. We hold a torch that should be held high in this world no matter where we go, even if we are surrounded by Christian nurses in a Baptist hospital. The world is full of darkness, pain, and sorrow and only we have the answer. We should be holding that torch up high.

I don't ever want to hear that someone didn't know I was saved, washed in the Blood, filled with the Holy Ghost, and glorifying God. I want to shine that Light wherever I go. If I am not primed and ready to shine in easy places like a Baptist hospital, how will I find the courage to hold up the torch in those dark places where proclaiming your faith can get you killed?

The problem is generated from our view of ourselves. If we are full of ourselves -- our problems and our successes, our triumphs and our miseries – then we don't easily notice the needs of others. It's when we look over that personal wall we have around us to see the plight that others have that we can reach through that wall and touch a person's soul and make a difference in their life that could result in changing their eternal destiny.

I'm not good at that. Most people aren't. We have to consciously press our attention to the world around us, especially when we are holding a torch in our hand that can change the world.

It is only when we begin to make the effort to reach through that wall that we will see the bricks begin to crumble and the path to reaching the lost becomes clear and easy. Not before. We have to make the first step. God will give us the power, but we have to make the effort first. "Draw nigh to God," James 4:8 says, "and he will draw nigh to you."

When we don't, the consequences can be eternal.

"Charity ... seeketh not her own." (1st Corinthians 13:5)

Cognitive Dissonance

This morning I was reminded of a pastor I met in northern Nigeria some years ago who would go out without any money and plant churches. He had few resources, but he would raise the church up until it was healthy and firm, and then he would go off to another area to plant the next church. When I met him, he had already planted several churches this way, taking nothing for himself for money or support. He just went on by faith.

I am also reminded of another pastor that I ministered with who was given $50,000 as an offering from a UK-based church. Instead of buying himself a nice home or car, he used that money to build the foundations for over 150 churches across northern Uganda. He remained dirt poor and didn't have the money to finish many of those buildings, but they were functioning churches nonetheless, and that was what mattered for the hundreds of people that worshipped God in them.

I know several men and women of God like that.

Is this what I see here in the modern church world in America where the preachers expound more about blessings and prosperity than the sufferings of the Cross and the fear of God? They proudly display their wealth across television networks as a sign of their blessings from God. I am tired of hearing that it's not the money, but the <u>love</u> of money that is the root of all evil, all the while using that same scripture as an excuse to pursue more wealth. As the scripture says, they think "gain is godliness" (1 Tim. 6:5). But the admonition is to turn away from them because they are destitute of the truth.

And as the shepherd goes, so goes the flock. Our church world has, in many areas, taken on a worldly sheen that even the unsaved can recognize. They can see it, and we can't. Small wonder that so many refuse to darken the doors of any church. They don't see anything in the modern church world that they want.

Do you see what I am seeing? Can you feel that something in the church world is just not right, but you're not quite sure what it is? Does it seem difficult to pick out any one thing that you can point to as wrong, but still there is that feeling that something is off? A friend of mine calls it cognitive dissonance.

How did we get so far off course? This was not the way the church was a couple of generations ago. Certainly, we've seen men of

God that were blessed and enjoyed a certain amount of wealth, but not to the degree of the lavish lifestyles we see today. The difference that is so startling is not about the money, but the attitude.

Are we focused on the comforts of the crown or the sufferings of the Cross? Are the rewards we pursue measured in coins or in souls? Are we trying to get our rewards now, or lay them up for Eternity?

Paul said that he would not glory except in the cross, "by whom the world is crucified unto me, and I unto the world." (Gal 6:14) The apostle John agreed and warned us to not love the world, neither the things in the world, for if we did, the love of the father would not be in us. (1John 2:15). Even James told us that friendship with the world is enmity with God. (James 4:4)

So how did so many of us lose our bearings? Perhaps it is a matter of what we are focused on.

I see so many Christians in the churches dive off into their own ministries, which seems encouraging until I notice that they are running around ministering to each other and have forgotten the commission that was given to them to go unto the lost. They seem to be run more like a corporate business than an outreach by faith. Few are willing to give up the security of a paycheck to run off into the bush to plant a church with nothing in their pocket. Neither do many feel the call to sacrifice everything they have in life just so they can go.

Is this generation focused only on their own lives, what they want, and how they want it, rather than the crucified sacrifice that fueled our forefathers? Is it all about us and how we want it instead of allowing God to take you through the valleys of death so He can strip the "you" out of you? Or are we like Gideon, who refused to compromise with a worldly church, but instead, threshed his wheat in secret by the winepress of God, away from the religious ways of a carnal church.

Paul echoes Isaiah as he cried out for us to come out from among them and be separate people unto the Lord. (2nd Corinthians 6:17, Isaiah 52:11). Just as he was preparing to go to Calvary, Jesus told His followers "ye are not of the world". If you were, as John says later, the world would hear you (1st John 4:5,6). Peter says we are supposed to escape the pollutions of this world by cutting off our desire to be like them. (2 Peter 2:20)

Is this what I see in the modern church world today? Is this the example that is set by our affluent clergy and wealthy congregations? Or, is this the same spirit that led the children of Israel to worship golden calves at the foot of Mount Sinai?

Choose a path. I don't believe you can have both. The deception of the world is too strong to dabble in. Like skating on thin ice to see how far you can go, you may not find out until it is too late.

"Woe to them that are at ease in Zion, and trust in the mountain of Samaria ... That lie upon beds of ivory, and stretch themselves upon their couches, and eat the lambs out of the flock ... and anoint themselves with the chief ointments: but they are not grieved for the affliction of Joseph." (Amos 6:1-6)

Humility – the breakfast of champions.

Abraham had it when he declared he was nothing but dust and ashes. So did Jacob as he stood before Pharaoh and blessed the most powerful king on earth as a greater would bless a lesser. As a matter of fact, every hero of God had it, but it didn't always look like it.

David had it; Saul did not. Why? Because with Saul, it was always about Saul, but with David, it was always about God. That's why Saul ultimately failed and why David had the boldness as a young boy to stand and mock Goliath and later on, with two of his comrades to stand and defeat an entire army in a field of barley. (1 Chron. 11:13-14)

Moses was the meekest man on earth, but you never saw him wilt before any of the bullies in the congregation. He was too afraid of God to be worried about some puffed-up rebels like Korah, Dathan, and Abiram.

Elijah had it. You could hear it in his voice when he stood before the king of Israel and cried about "the Lord God, before whom I stand." He feared God, not the king. It gave him the boldness to call down fire from heaven. And nobody got in his way when he started hacking the priests and prophets of Baal into pieces.

Josiah had it when they had found the lost book of the Law, and, in fear and repentance, cleansed the Temple and slaughtered all the sodomites and false idol worshippers. But then, he lost it later on when he thought he could take on Pharaoh who was trying to pass through Judah on his way to Babylon.

Peter had to learn it the hard way while John seemed to take to it naturally.

Paul learned it on the road to Damascus. It's what kept him going when he faced all the beatings and persecution that he went through.

Jesus had it. He was the essence of humility, yet he never backed down from the devil or any of the religious leaders that came against him, even whipping them out of the Temple. His boldness came from his fear of God. Hebrews 5:7 tells us that He "was heard in that he feared". That gave him, not only his power and authority in God, but also his humility.

Humility is meekness toward God, not toward man. It is not a sense of inferiority where we stand hat-in-hand, staring at our shoes while we mumble out weak apologies for our faith. Humility is the power in God that is gained when we step out of ourselves – our flesh, our intelligence, our pride, our idea of who and what we are – and step into the mantle of the Holy Spirit and the shoes of Christ.

Yes, they are big shoes! And no, you can't fill them in your own power! It is only when you yield completely to the lordship of Christ that you are able to walk in them. That requires a broken, crucified walk in God – crucified unto the world and to yourself, broken from your selfish pride and desires for recognition, and purged from your own ways until you become an empty vessel of transparent glass. Only then can you be filled with God's power as you become invisible so that He, and He alone, gets the glory.

And with that, you enter into an authority and power in God that is devoid of all flesh so that you may work the works of God in true humility and humbleness of mind.

> *"The sacrifices of God are a broken spirit: a broken and a contrite heart, O God, thou wilt not despise." (Psalms 57:17)*
>
> *"Humble yourselves in the sight of the Lord, and he shall lift you up." (James 4:10)*

"If my people, which are called by my name, shall humble themselves, and pray, and seek my face, and turn from their wicked ways; then will I hear from heaven, and will forgive their sin, and will heal their land."
(2nd Chronicles 7:14)

Christmas Gifts

Ah, it's Christmas again! There's no snowflakes or frosty air down here in Texas, so that old-fashioned Christmas feeling is not quite the same as it was when I was a kid in New England, but then Christmas isn't about snow or Santa and Christmas trees either. We may have over-commercialized Christmas so that it doesn't have that same old feeling it used to, but it's still Christmas.

I have always believed that God honors this time with that certain feeling in the air that is different from the rest of the year. True, Jesus was not born in December. I believe the Bible points to the first day of the Feast of Tabernacles as the day he was born, and the Festival of Lights or Hanauka for when he was conceived, but I'm not so sure that celebrating the exact day is all that important to God. If it was, wouldn't He have told us?

Neither am I worried about Christmas trees being a form of idolatry. Or Santa and the elves, or tinsel, or Grandma's fruitcake from last year. This is Christmas. Do we have to make an intense, super-spiritual controversy over it? Can we just enjoy it for what it is and celebrate the birth and advent of our Savior?

Since we're talking about getting in the Christmas spirit of things, how about giving and receiving gifts? I have some gift requests from God that I would like for Christmas. He may not be able to fit them under the tree, and He may have trouble trying to gift wrap them, but here is my list:

Lord, I would like wisdom, understanding, and knowledge – the knowledge of Your Word so that I can believe the right things and know the truths that are buried in it, the understanding to be able to know how that knowledge fits into everything, and the wisdom to know how to use it to win souls.

Of course, that comes from reading the Bible every day, so Lord, along with that, I need an intense hunger to read the Bible like a starving man eating the Bread of Life. And while you're at it, could you also make me so thirsty for intense, prevailing prayer that I can't breathe without it?

That's just my Christmas stocking-stuffers. I have some other requests for the big presents under the tree. Let me start with the Anointing. I need that Presence on me so that it is dripping off me wherever I go. I want to be immersed in it, saturated, swimming in it. So much so that when I pray with or over anyone, they will feel the tingling of your touch when I pray. I want them to know you are not only real but that they themselves can have a real and immediate access to you on a deeply personal level.

And for my next present (can I have another one, Lord?), I want power. I mean real, Holy Ghost power – <u>u</u><u>nprecedented</u> power – power to raise the dead and heal whomsoever I lay hands on. But most of all, I want the power to preach your Word under the anointing of the Holy Ghost so that it will pierce hearts, set them on fire, and inspire a generation to rise up and shine a Light in this world.

I also want authority to cast out devils with one word. I don't want to argue with them. When I say, "Get out!", I want them to get out! Authority like that only comes from the fear of the Lord, so please heap that on me also. Since the Bible says that the fear of the Lord is wisdom, and James says that if we ask for wisdom, You'll give it liberally, then pour it out on me, Lord!

In return, I don't have much to offer. All I can give is myself, weak and faulty as I am. I give you my pride and desire for recognition, my gluttony and lusts, my fears and darkness, my suspicions, accusations, and hatreds – all the ugly stuff that I can dredge up from the dark recesses of my heart. Lord I give you what I am and all that I have. I will do whatsoever you ask and go wherever you send me – I just have one final request:

(Do we have room for one more? This is the most important one, Lord, so we <u>have</u> to make room for this one.)

Dear God, please, in the name of Jesus and everything that is holy and good, please, please, please … send revival.

Inspiration to Keep Going

> *"And I heard a voice from heaven saying unto me, Write, Blessed are the dead which die in the Lord from henceforth: Yea, saith the Spirit, that they may rest from their labors; and their works do follow them." Revelations 14:13*

That's exactly how I feel sometimes. I'm looking forward to dying so I can get a break. But I don't want any work following me. I've had enough work to last for a lifetime!

Have you ever felt like that? Everything is a struggle, and nothing ever seems to go smoothly? It's like you're pushing a cart through Life and the road is always going uphill. When do we get to sit on that cart and ride it downhill?

I realize that work is what we got out of the Garden of Eden. Whether it's fair or not, we have inherited our ancestor's foolishness. (Thanks a lot, Dad.) Did God allow this to happen so that we would appreciate Heaven when we finally got there? If that's the case, then I'm ready, Lord. You can beam me up anytime.

Maybe that's why the Bible says we need a vision. We would perish without one because we'd have nothing to strive for, no reason to push through the hard stuff, no light to give us a direction. We need something to get us through those times when we feel like we have the best product in the world (and we do), but nobody wants it, and you are just beating your head against a wall. It's times like that when we need those anointed people who light a torch of faith and hope that inspires us to keep going.

David was like that. In one of his many times of darkness, he wrote in Psalms 37,

"I have seen the wicked in great power, and spreading himself like a green bay tree, Yet he passed away, and, lo, he was not."

Your time will come. The superficial never last long, and the chaff always gets blown away, but that which you have planted and worked so hard for in the Lord will follow you one day.

Does it seem dark and fearful right now? Does it seem like God has forgotten you and is a million miles away? David answered again,

"Yea, though I walk through the valley of the shadow of death, I will fear no evil: for thou art with me."

The nature of faith is that you face the direction that your heart wants to go in and you choose to believe. The inspiration to keep going springs forth from the seeds of that faith that you planted.

Keep going. You're almost there.

"They that sow in tears shall reap in joy. He that goeth forth and weepeth, bearing precious seed, shall doubtless come again with rejoicing, bringing his sheaves with him."
(Psalms 126: 5,6)

One-Way Prayer

Do you ever feel like you're banging your head against the wall when you pray and not getting anything back? Are there times when you wonder if your prayers are getting anywhere or if He is just simply quietly listening, contemplating His next move?

When I first got saved, I hated going into the prayer room. Everyone at our church had to take a prayer hour that they were responsible for every day. It was great training, but it was the hard part of my day.

I would go into the prayer room each day with dread because I didn't know what to say for sixty minutes. I just didn't have a request list that long. So I would end up repeating the same things over and over, and then after what seemed a sufficient amount of time, I would move on to the next request. It was as if I was supposed to follow some organized format of placing my request on the table and hoping that somehow God would notice it, stop by and maybe read it. Then maybe He would consider it, perhaps talk it over with some of the angels and see if it was any good, and then either answer it, reject it, or put it in the "Later" pile.

Sometimes I would sit there and wonder what all that stupid repetition sounded like to God. Here is the most intelligent entity of the universe suffering through this babble that sounded like it was directed to a moron. Did He ever get tired of it? I sure would, and I wasn't anywhere near as smart as God.

The truth is, I just didn't know how to pray.

I would love to tell you that some incredible light bulb went off and I finally saw the light. It didn't, and neither did I. There was no epiphany that all of a sudden changed my whole perspective. I think I just got tired of trying too hard.

It was when I finally surrendered, that it all came together for me. At that point, the door opened to real communion with God, and when it did, I was flooded with a world of possibility.

God doesn't live on a one-way street. The traffic flows both ways with Him. If it doesn't, then you might be banging on the wrong door.

You can get advice on how to pray from just about anywhere. Lots of well-meaning folks would love to tell you how it works. But that's what works for them. It's like telling someone to just have faith. How do you "just have faith"?

No, prayer – the deep kind that pierces the

heavens and moves God – is a personal thing. It has to be real, not something that comes packaged in a book or some program to follow, otherwise, you'd be flapping your wings, but never able to get off the ground.

Prayer has to be personal – just between you and God – it has to be real, and you have to want it bad enough to go get it yourself.

Full of Surprises

> *"Forasmuch then as God gave them the like gift as he did unto us, who believed on the Lord Jesus Christ; what was I, that I could withstand God?"* Acts 11:17

God is full of surprises.

No sooner do you have everything figured out, and He goes and does something different. It keeps you on your toes. It also keeps you humble.

Peter had a lot of surprises that day, and it turned upside-down a lot of what he and the other Apostles thought was pretty standard doctrine. Here God not only had turned to the Gentiles, but He baptized them in the Holy Ghost before they ever made it to the water! John's baptism was officially over.

Thank God that, instead of resisting the Holy Spirit like we see so much of today in our plethora of doctrinal debates, the Apostles rejoiced in this new move of God.

Actually, it wasn't new. God was still the same – they just didn't see it coming. It was all written in God's Word long before any of these guys were born. You see, God reveals His Plan in His own time, and you never know when He will step into a whole new thing that you weren't expecting. Better to just shut up and let God do the driving.

In these times when following prophesies about the Last Days excites the religious imagination, we see a lot of would-be scholars running around trying to figure out the Word of God. Carnal attempts to analyze the spiritual, however, are like using an Ouija Board to find directions to New York City. There are just some things that you have to trust God to lead you by the Spirit of God to get you there. Try anything else, and you're bound to get lost and end up in Podunk, Mississippi.

But we never stop trying, do we? And in our attempt to make ourselves theologically correct, we find ourselves stuck on one idea or another, and we will fight to the bitter end to defend them lest we be found to be wrong. The truth is, our little pea brains understand so little that we often miss the whole point.

Why not just let God reveal it to you?

I have found over the past 53 years that, the more I learn, the less I understand. There is so much more to God's Truth than I ever imagined possible when I first got saved. And I haven't made it to Heaven yet! Wow, who knows what surprises are in store for us up there?

So while many others are scurrying around squabbling over points of doctrine and sequence of end-time events, I'll just stick to the basics. You can't go wrong with the basics.

When the rest of you guys figure it all out, send me a Postcard. I'll be out fishing somewhere.

"Knowledge puffeth up, but charity edifeth" (1st Corinthians 8:1)

Email from an African Evangelist

I received this email from an African evangelist:

From: samwel miroro
[mailto:samwel2000miroro@gmail.com]
Sent: Wednesday, November 18, 2015 2:15 AM

"We are experiencing one problem, brother Dale. Once we preach to people and take them to different churches, they come out saying that they do not feel like being there. We are even confused for pastors because they do not follow-up with these souls. We need your advice. May God bless you."

My answer:

"If I am hearing you correctly, you have the worldwide common problem of dead churches. Most of the active churches today were birthed in revival years ago. Revival is more of a revolution from the old dead religious orders than something that "revives" them. Once a body is dead, you cannot bring it back to life. The answer – God's answer – is a revival in a new movement of the Holy Spirit.

While you and your group of believers may be alive and in the Spirit, based on what you have told me, it sounds like the churches that you're trying to plug these new believers into are dead. Jesus told us in John 6 that it is God that draws souls to repentance. (John 6:44) The Spirit of God is the active element in the winning of the lost. Therefore, if souls are not getting saved in your church, or in your case, once plugged in, they run out of there, then it is a simple step of logic to assume that the Spirit of God is not working there.

The solution? You have two that I can see: <u>1) Take them to another church</u>. You will have to pray, search, and test the spirits to find one. You will find plenty that sound good and look good, but the depth and fire of any church are determined by their dedication to prayer and reading God's Word. Hear me carefully – smiling faces do not indicate spiritual depth. Great music does not mean true worship. Good intentions don't mean spiritual righteousness.

Is there an obvious presence of serious prayer in their church? Do they gather together as a church to cry out to God? The furnace for any church is always the weekly prayer meeting. How many people show up, and do they pray with strong passion? Or is it a weak response to

Holy Ghost conviction and a poor excuse for serious prayer? Just as your prayer life determines your place in God, so does a church's corporate prayer life determine theirs.

You will find churches that do not even have a prayer room to speak of, whose Wednesday night prayer meetings have been canceled for lack of interest, and yet they will consider themselves a "praying church" because, for 5 minutes during Sunday services, they pray for others. How can the Holy Spirit work without prayer? Avoid these places because, as you have seen, they will kill that brand-new excitement in these freshly born-again souls. Don't look at appearances; look for substance. Look for the presence of the Spirit of God. If you can feel it, He is there; if you cannot, then look somewhere else.

2) Start your own church. Many times in the past, the Lord would begin a new work because of these very same conditions. You're winning souls but you have no place to safely put them. You can feel the responsibility that is upon you. Like the Good Samaritan who handed the wounded man to the innkeeper, you want to make sure that he is well taken care of. If you cannot find a place that is full of the same fire that birthed them into the Kingdom, then maybe

you will have to start your own.

I understand the difficulty that implies. Like you, I travel from one church to the next. Once a fire is started, I can only hope that the leadership will continue to fan the flames while I head to the next church. But you may be facing a little different situation than mine in that as an evangelist, you are preaching to and gathering new souls. They are now your responsibility to make sure they are taken care of. Maybe, just maybe, He is going to use you to start a new work where new souls can be raised up in the fear of the Lord, the depth of the Word of God, and the fire of the Holy Ghost.

It will be hard. So is everything we have to face in this battle for souls. But, if it is truly the will of God, then expect Him to present the solution, the means, and the opportunities.

The greatest problem we have in the Church today is our lack of desperation to seek the face of God. We just don't need Him as much as we used to. Our blessings are killing us. As a result, our efforts to plumb spiritual depths are anemic. We hardly do any serious reading of God's Word. Oh, we'll read all these <u>other</u> books – Christian self-help manuals, opinions and personal revelations and advice, and carnally-based efforts at theology – but we won't put forth a determined effort to get our answers from the depth of His Word. It's like the children of Israel that sent Moses up into the mountain to meet God while they chose to stay at the foot of Mt. Sinai. We'll pay someone else to do the work while we will wait for the next book to come out. It is a form of substitutionary faith. We just aren't hungry enough to be desperate for God, but that is what God wants before He will honor us with revival.

The other problem, very much like the above, is that we have come to rely upon theological scholasticism rather than spiritual edification and revelation. Our Bible colleges have pushed an agenda upon us that, first, you have to go to college to preach the Gospel because you have to learn all this seemingly intelligent theological education to minister in the Spirit. What hogwash! Eating of the Tree of the Knowledge of Good and Evil does not give you wisdom – it only makes you <u>desire</u> it.

But to be carnally-minded is death (Rom. 8:6). That process to obtain carnal wisdom is fueled by pride, whereas to eat off the Tree of Life, you have to humble yourself and allow God to work through you as a broken, totally surrendered vessel. What did God tell us? Fear God and keep His commandments for this is the whole duty of man. As for carnal theological efforts, He tells us that there is <u>no end</u> to the making of many books, and much study (carnal study) is a weariness of the <u>flesh</u>. Hmmm. Let's see. Which tree should I eat from?

What about prayer? Without a desperate, consuming need, our passion will dissipate into routine obedience. We no longer need God for our healings, our daily food, our finances, or our well-being. No, we are like the Church of Laodicea – we have arrived and are comfortable. Our prayer life can now be relegated to a more mundane part of our lives. We spend a few minutes during our "quiet time with Jesus" in "conversational prayer", thinking that somehow we have done our duty. But it is passion that pierces the heavens, not passiveness. Desperation gets God's attention, not manners. If you want it to rain, you have to pray like Elijah! You cannot approach the Throne of God in timidity and fearfulness and expect to get an answer from God. That only shows a lack of faith in the power of the blood of Jesus. Holy boldness, which is generated by righteousness and the fear of the Lord, is what breaks down every barrier to victory. Our forefathers prayed with a passion and furor that clamored to the Throne of God and refused to back down until

God answered. Today, people are afraid to pray like that. No wonder there is no stirring in our churches!

Am I exaggerating? If I am, then please explain to me where are the miracles, the altars packed with lost souls, the evidence of God's power, and the manifest presence of the Holy Ghost? If all is so well with the church, then where is the revival? Gideon had the same question, but at least he realized that the problem had been created when they had let the Amalekites take over their land. We, on the other hand, have let the world into our church, and we celebrate it!

You are faced with a battle. Only God has the answer for you. Remember, these are His souls, not yours. He will provide, but you have to seek His face with all your heart to get the answer. It is your prime responsibility. If you won't do it, who will?

Gideon

"...and his son Gideon threshed wheat by the winepress... (Judges 6:11)

Israel, at this time, was going through a terrible time of persecution. The enemy had periodically destroyed the harvest to the point that the people of God were starving. People were hiding in caves and dens, and those who were not were in fear for their lives. The judgments of God were heavy upon the Israelites because, instead of separating themselves from the idolaters of the land, they had embraced them. The resulting oppression left them with little or no hope.

But Gideon was threshing his wheat by the winepress of God. That was the place where there was still hope to reap the Bread of Life. There was hope in that covered, hidden place where the wine of the Spirit of God was trodden out. The Lord saw that hope and sent out the call of God to him.

The story of Gideon is one of the great victories of God. The Lord chose someone who was little in his own sight to stand in the power of God and restore the presence and greatness of

God in the land. What an incredible victory! Gideon leaned upon the Lord and trusted in Him to bring about what flesh could never have accomplished.

Warnings are throughout the Word of God that there would be terrible spiritual desolation in the last days. We see it in Amos, Joel, Isaiah, Ezekiel, Revelations, and Thessalonians, to just name a few. Even Jesus warned us about it. Although our church bulletins tell us about the wonderful things that are happening, we still remain hungry and starving for a great move of God in our churches. Where are the glories that we have heard about in the revivals of times past? The Book of James says, "...the body without the spirit is dead." Is that not also true about our churches? The enemy has destroyed the harvest and sucked the faith and hope from our churches for a restoration of a great and mighty outpouring of God. As a result, we remain sedate and satisfied with what we have and begin to believe that this is all God has for us.

But there are those who plow their hope in the soil beside the winepress of God. We huddle close to the place where the Spirit of the Lord is pressed out and look to the heavens for the increase. Surely, the Lord has not forgotten His people.

When the Lord raises up His ministers to burn in a fire of defiance, there will always be resistance, but the Lord knows those who are willing to stand in the power of God to proclaim victory and deliverance. There comes a time when you have had enough of the oppression, when you're tired of being considered second-rate in society, when you're sick and tired of being comfortable with "church as usual", and when you are ready to stand for the honor of God regardless of what the cost may be.

When the fire of God is flowing through your veins, there is nothing that can stop you. And once that fire is kindled, it will grow into a blaze that will consume every enemy that stands in the way. Send down an outpouring of the Holy Ghost, O Lord, that will shake the very foundations of the earth! Lord, we claim victory!

Thresh beside the winepress of God, come what may, and believe God for the greatest revival of all time. For surely it will come.

Visitations and Ignorance

I went knocking on doors today to invite people to church. They call it Visitation down here in Texas.

One guy hadn't gone to church in ages. But hey, he was okay. He still considered himself a church member even though he couldn't remember when the last time was that he had been there. Besides, he said, he didn't come because the seats were too uncomfortable for his wife. We had cushioned chairs, but she needed the old wooden pews for some reason. Go figure.

His neighbor was different. No, he didn't go to church anywhere, and he probably wasn't going anytime soon. Yeah, his brother got saved, and he knew it was real, but it just wasn't for him.

What are you supposed to say to these folks? The cushions hurt your back so you're not going to church? I couldn't help thinking about the people in Africa who would walk for 10 to 12 hours just to come to our revival services. And then sleep on the ground on a bamboo mat for three days just so they could hear the Word of God. But you're not going to come unless the church has the right kind of chairs?

Or his neighbor who knows that salvation is a real experience but consciously turns his face away so he can ignore it. What is he thinking? That if he doesn't look at it, it will dissolve? God will go away if you ignore Him? Hell won't burn if you wish it away?

Unfortunately, these responses are so common that I would venture that most people fall into one category or the other. Either you convince yourself that, because you are a churchgoer, you don't have to worry about your eternal destiny anymore, or you convince yourself that if you don't look at the truth, it will go away. Both are self-induced delusions.

But whose fault is it that so many people are like these two?

I am not making a case for church just for church's sake, but I do believe that the church is the place that we are supposed to gather to as believers, where we get nourished, reproved, and inspired. When you cut yourself off from the hierarchy of believers that God has set up, then you are setting yourself up for a fall.

But many would say that the churches are not what they are supposed to be anymore; that they are dead in comparison to what they once were. Agreed, but will that excuse hold water when you stand before God? It was the Church's fault?

Adam tried to blame Eve in the same way. It didn't work for him; do you really think it will work for you?

Maybe the churches have failed you. So what? Then go find a group of believers like yourself, or start your own church, but for heaven's sake, don't stick your head in the sand and ignore it. The problem will not go away if you don't do something about it.

Yes, we need a revival. Desperately. I don't think many people realize how badly. We need a revolution in our churches. We have become like the children of Israel who spent 400 years in slavery. Why so long? Because they got used to the slavery and settled into their bondage. It wasn't until God, in His mercy, sent a Pharaoh who was so bad that he started killing their babies that they began to cry out to God for deliverance.

But when they cried unto God in their desperation, He heard them and sent a mighty deliverance.

Are we at that point yet? Or will God have to send something so terrible that it will make 9/11 look small in comparison? If He does, it will be in His mercy to bring us to our knees. Only then will He be able to answer our cries for help.

Revival does not come cheap and it does not fall out of the skies. It has to be sought for with all your heart. But it is always worth the price.

The alternative is Hell.

About the Author

Dalen Garris has been in ministry since 1970 during the Jesus Movement in California. In 1997, he began a radio broadcast that ultimately spread to dozens of countries, from Israel and Saudi Arabia to Africa and the Philippines. His program, *Fire in the Hole*, was selected for broadcast four times a week for several years across North America on the Sky Angel network as the Voice of Jerusalem.

A newspaper column followed, for which he has written over 700 articles, which have been published in local newspapers and Christian magazines in several countries. He has also written over a dozen books and several booklets.

Since 2004, he has been lighting the fires of revival in churches spread across sub-Saharan Africa. During the course of 17 years, he has preached in over 1,000 churches and has seen hundreds of them set on fire and explode with growth, and hundreds of new ones planted across Africa.

Hundreds of people have been supernaturally healed during the healing lines that so often sprang up during these revival meetings, and tens of thousands have been saved. And the fires are still burning.

Because of his work across Africa, Dalen Garris was awarded an honorary Doctorate in 2017 by the Northwestern Christian University of Florida.

Dr. Garris currently lives with Cindy, his wife of over 43 years, in Waxahachie and is still heavily involved with churches across Africa.

His pressing hope is in seeing this powerful move of God in Africa ignite us here in America to see those same revival services that made such an explosion in Africa. He believes that this upcoming generation will be the Gideon Generation that will usher in this last, great revival that he has preached about for so many years.

Brother Dale, as he is known across Africa, has settled in Waxahachie, Texas, with his wife and three grown daughters and their children. You can contact him and find his pamphlets, books, videos, and podcasts at www.RevivalFire.org.

If you would like him to speak at your church or organization, please contact us for times and schedules. We do not charge, nor will we ever charge, to preach the Gospel anywhere in the world.

He is willing to take this message anywhere people are hungry for a God-given, Holy Ghost revival.

Books by Dalen Garris:

Available at: www.Revivalfre.org/books

Doctrinal Issues
- Four Steps to Revival
- Do You Have Eternal Security?
- Standing in the Gap
- Two Covenants
- Fire in the Hole

Revival Campaigns
- The Kenya Diaries
- A Trumpet in Nigeria
- A Scent of Rain
- Into the Heart of Darkness
- Fire and Rain
- Revival Campaigns in Africa – 2019
- The Battle for Nigeria
  - A Light in the Bush
- A Match in Dry Grass
- Finishing What We Started

A Voice in the Wilderness series:
- vol. 1, The Journey Begins
- vol. 2, the Early Years
- vol. 3, Prophet Rising
- vol. 4, Revival in the Wings

vol. 5, Sound of an Abundance of Rain
vol. 6, Watchman, What of the Night?
vol. 7, Mud and Heroes
vol. 8, Ashes in the Morning
vol. 9, Shaking the Olive Tree
vol. 10, Winds of Change
vol. 11, A Final Call

Booklets by Dalen Garris

Available at: www.Revivalfire.org/booklets/

A Volcano in Cape Verde
Tanzania, 2011
Nigeria, 2012
Planting a Seed in Liberia
A Whisper in the Wind
Calvinism Critique

RevivalFire Ministries

PO Box 822
Waxahachie, TX 75168
dale@revivalfire.org

http://RevivalFire.org

www.ingramcontent.com/pod-product-compliance
Lightning Source LLC
Chambersburg PA
CBHW070449050426
42451CB00015B/3412